To Rico, a very beatiful Queen I had the pleasure of [...] along my journey

WINDOWS TO MY SOUL

By

Johnny E. Osby II

ALL RIGHTS RESERVED

Printed in the United States of America

PGL Publishing
Po Box 22084
Akron, Ohio 44302

Dedication

This book is dedicated to the creator for blessing me with the gift of a visionary. This book is also dedicated to my mother; Marian (Mother Wright) McCullough and my father; Johnny E. Osby, for their role in the production of my incarnate spirit. To my children: Tashayla J Osby, Johnny C. Osby, Johnny E. Osby III, Jontre E. Osby and Jalisa Massey. I leave this book as a legacy for you to be proud of as well as a blue print for your lives. I pray that you will continue to seek knowledge, wisdom and spirituality infinitely. I love you. To friends and extended family; with this book, I offer a percentage of myself that may have been previously unbeknown to you. With that being said, I will now allow the creator to use me and guide you through the ***Windows To My Soul.***

A journey through the eyes of a man fulfilling his purpose in life

Acknowledgements

I would like to extend special thanks to my friends/brothers; Bobby Jackson, Terrance D. Shelton, Kevin Rice and Chester Starks, for propelling me into my purpose and destiny. Harambe!!! I also would like to acknowledge my best friends ; Perry Keith Jeffries III a.k.a., *The Ambassador Of Night Life,* DeAndre Karim and Cameron Mack, for being there like real friends should. I appreciate it and I owe you big time. To the mother of my children: Charmaine Stewart, thank you for being patient with my demeanor. I know that I'm one of a kind … most geniuses are. To my Upstatecats family; Rob Lee, Schizo, Glory, Nilez and Dee we here man. What up Fly Ty and the Rockboy family. Kelvin, I ain't forgot about you boy. To my bra; JoVon Carter, I'm holdin' you down out here fam! Always and forever…word up! Lots of love to LaTron and Latroy Larkins, Daryll "Flight" Washington, Ed "Buck" Murray Mike Aktive, Kyro, Leidi and to all my moms; Mrs. Jeffries, Mrs. Karim & Mrs. Dixie. What up, Geisha, Special thanks to Marcy Ronen for the commercials. Special thanks to Jerry Rowland and Audley McGill, Livewire Graphics, Buronni Fashions, 3S's Apparel, Central Hower Alumni Forever, Monroe Community College, PlayGround Legends Inc, King of the 90's Parties, North Star Multi Media! Mothers on a Mission

(MOMS). Akron, Ohio and Rochester, NY! Stand up!
One!

TABLE OF CONTENTS

THE POWER

Loneliness is the heart whispering for love
Love is the long distance carrier for GOD
which connects GOD to love and love to your loved
ONE

Mistakes are forgiven and erased by love
To love is GOD
GOD is love…GOD is the personality of love

Love is undefined by those who call it an action
You can't act love…you can only feel love
Love comes when you least expect
Love hides when you neglect it

True love never leaves
Every time you think of true love
it's hard to breathe…to breathe is love

To find true love one must love GOD
Love themselves and
love their situations before they can truly
love someone else

THE WINDOWS TO MY SOUL

Love is life
Love is always there
Love is heart felt

Even in the after life
love sheds light

The strength of love will scare people away
Sometimes the strength of love embraces souls and never
allows them to get away

UNSTOPPABLE PEACE

I'm two months behind in bills
It feels as if financially I'm climbing hills

The opposite of a daughter so I'm shining still
Frustration over comes my desire
Depression, stress is out to kill
me…my will…and my fire

The source within transcends my abilities
to look within and find tranquility
within me

SACRAFICE

I've been an eye witness to a sibling's evil stare
with absolutely no care emotion wasn't there

Relationships valued like an invisible masterpiece
where the frigid air smelled like blood

Directly from the heart…that spelled out *grudge*
As the heat of my temper met the forming clouds
of dark love
Lightning struck
Thunder crackled
Rain poured

I wonder is it worth seeing you any more
Daughter versus Mother
I'd referred to many times before

All I could hear was a small voice
saying give it to me
Yes…my Lord

2 MUCH MAN

It took Big Mama's death
to bring us face to face
From Ohio to Mississippi
Same name different birthplaces

My visit was awkward and quite strange
I felt the love of my people
but didn't know their names

My arrival was anticipated
but my approach was agitated
My heart and soul said home
The child in me said I'm grown

Dad or Mr. Johnny
Or you weak ass niggah or call my mommy
Now this road I must cross alone

I humbled myself to avoid the wrong reaction
He spoke like a dad to me
I smiled with satisfaction

The man in me could not give him the satisfaction
of assuming he had raised me

THE WINDOWS TO MY SOUL

So I ignored him respectfully thinking
I just can't honor your position
cause you didn't practice to keep it
plus your life style is not recommended
nor healthy or tradition

So instantaneously I forgave you
I thanked you for what I'd been missing
cause had you been around I might have followed you
and continued a generation of soldiers
who think just like you

Thank you for your genes and the access to ancestors
who came before you
I'm not mad anymore
I'm here for you

DAD

BEAUTY IS UGLY

Miraculously I was sent from a spiritual
existence to the physical prenatal
not knowing my life was destined to be fatal
As a young soldier naive to prejudices
and what white folk' had planned for me

A hard working laborer…price negotiable
depending on if I could bob and weave
the noose…I mean the laws conceived
Like a dumb ass I thought we were FREE
We were only as FREE as the
ancestors and elders taught us to be

Since Willie Lynch taught them to hate us
they don't want to teach
preach or reach for us
As we drown and destroy ourselves
land and children

Elders don't take responsibility for what they've given
And not given to their children to recycle
That's wise involuntarily enslaving us back to the pilgrim

My eyes see the irony when I go to church for inspiration
Church is not helping our generation
but preserving theirs

THE WINDOWS TO MY SOUL

Selfishly taking all knowledge
and wisdom to the grave
Involuntarily molding us into slaves
It would be nice to hear some historical factual
cultural events at church as well as biblical
My oracles convinced we still 3/5
of a human lacking history and culture
leaving certain people to prey like a vulture
over the decay of my culture and history

It'll be nice to know HIS-story
Life is beautiful as long as you realize
what *they* can do to you

Find and fulfill your purpose
Correct some generational wrongs
Your parents did the best they could
with the resources exported from the hood

While they imported drugs, beer, liquor, tobacco and
guns for good marketing strategy
Go ahead…have fun

Unaware of the generational preparation
and projections mentally and physically infesting
I mean investing in our downfall

I stand as an imported African in America
stripped of my history and culture
I'm an
African American
Black
Negro
Niggah
and what the hell ever with my head held high
Overcoming every obstacle they sent to me
because we're here collectively for a reason

Whether it be in this life or the next
I will play my part in understanding
Why we Africans are left

I'll never forget the Africans
who sold our ancestors to the Europeans

It's business…never personal
"the American way"

HOOP DREAMS

Fifth grade was the year
I began to understand my existence
To breathe, live and love basketball

Everyday before school, during school and after school
Left hand, right hand, between the legs, around the back
Free throws

Sixth grade came and I'm the man
Growth spurts took me to another level
A ballin' rebel labeled a big man
No time for nothing else

My status and stock was risen defense asking for help
I'm dunking now moving the crowd
Since the seventh to current my skills are certain
Put dough up its curtains

Hoop as allowed me to live my dreams
of playing in college
which led me to acquire knowledge
Opening doors often frustrated 'cause I didn't go pro
GOD knew something I don't know
He leads…I follow

A GRATEFUL CELEBRATION

Life is beautiful
Every second
Every minute
Every hour
Every day
Every week
Every year
All lives are beautiful
To see what each life brings
Another Queen another King
To see which ancestors
have reintroduced themselves
Life sings like a million angels
The soundtrack to your soul
produced by your spirit
leaving melodies to live by
Hear it
Recite it
with all your might

THE WINDOWS TO MY SOUL

C.O.P.S

Everybody's prejudice
Its human nature for one to
take care of its own first
but there's a curse and lack of equality

Historically policemen/cops were white
used to recapture runaway slaves
When captured they would hang
beat and even rape them

Historically policemen/cops
would spray blacks with fire hoses
Sending attack dogs on them

Historically policemen/cops
would racially profile us
Shoot us and night stick us

American documents state that slavery can be
implemented upon incarceration
80% of prisoners are African Americans

They've hired African Americans
as policeman/cops
Everybody's prejudice
It's human nature to take care of our own first

JOHNNY E. OSBY II

BAD FATHER

Nine months I dealt with
cravings
unstable emotions
attitudes
and household chores while working
That's not enough

I rubbed your belly
went to the store after hours
and promoted understanding
That's not enough

I was at the hospital like
I was supposed to be
for limitless hours
That's not enough

I taught my children how to be
respectful
courteous
open minded
and how to love family and others
That's not enough

I introduce my son to sports
dreams and culture

THE WINDOWS TO MY SOUL

I cut his hair and bonded with him
That's not enough

I never could do enough to amount
to the miracle of child birth
But for what its worth
I'm tired of you telling me I'm not doing enough
when you want stuff

I can't and won't have money
every time you ask
I can't and won't be able to watch the kids
every time you ask

I understand that as long as you're
the custodial parent
I'll never do enough

TRUE LOVE DON'T HURT

LOVE is two souls
communicating through telepathy
with one goal that only heaven holds
Walking together in harmony
down one road

Destinations are clear
divine passion and romance
slow dancing into the future
Practicing Karma Sutra
Nights electrifies ice
when incisions are precise

Pleasure is a slice of the ultimate dream
Rice and wedding bells are the ultimate team
Complimentary characteristics
enhances my personality
Together we make choices
Two individuals unifying life equally
Queen and King governing the Kingdom
No regrets
No anger
For your happiness
I'll sacrifice mine twice

THE WINDOWS TO MY SOUL

I KNOW...

I know what broke feels like
Living out of state
No money
No family
No food
and I made it happen

I know what broke feels like
Being grown as hell
Living at home with your mom
Sleeping on the floor in your old room
without a job

I know what broke feels like
Living with your woman
and can't pay the bills
Kids need shoes and milk
Making $6.50 an hour

I know what broke feel like
Having No job!
No hustles!
No help!

I know what broke feel like...Do you

JOHNNY E. OSBY II

MISCOMMUNICATION

I saw a young boy about 8 years old
watch fiends shoot-up in basements
Uncles smoking refer and drinking 40's
Labels Old English…Pool sticks had English
In school he barely knew English
So of course school wasn't interesting

The streets were full of grown people
who thought like him while growing up
Now society identifies them as thugs
At age 12 he began selling drugs and stealing bikes
Clothes and G.I Joes
Exposed to smoking primos
15 years old doing time
His best friend on the way to college
Dreams of playing professional football
Life on the line

They lived a couple houses away from each other
Even called each other brothers
from different mothers
Both grew up in the gutter
Dream chasing
Somewhere there must have been a
miscommunication

THE WINDOWS TO MY SOUL

BLINDED

In my life
I saw church girls turn into strippers
and college prospects turn to pie flippers

In my life
I saw peeps I went to high school with
not doing to good
I then saw broke katz turn crooked in the hood

In my life
I saw independent women turn into gold diggers
I then saw non-drinkers turn into Henny sippers

In my life
I saw my man face 20 years biddin' it
I then saw the man my girl cheated with

In my life
I then saw kinfolk smoke crack
And I then saw how sinful folk act

In my life
I then saw children killed and abandoned
I then saw us take life for granted

JOHNNY E. OSBY II

In my life
I then saw women who didn't know how to be wives
I then saw boys front like men in disguise

In my life
I then saw someone I love die slowly
I then saw my pain comforted through clouds of hydro

In my life
I then saw myself two cents from being a bum
I then saw the reactions from my heart being numb

In my life…In my life

THE WINDOWS TO MY SOUL

DEAD BROKE DAD

I would rather sacrifice 18 years
to make sure you live the rest of your years
without tears and fears

I know I don't call write or visit like I'm supposed to
but yet I'm always close to you
I haven't spent much time with you
however I put the rhyme in you

Hopefully the life and legacy I leave
exceeds the boundaries that life has laid on me

How can I teach you if I don't know knowledge of *self*
Sadly it had to be simultaneously and cost me my health
A small price to pay for your future

As a matter of fact you are the future so I invest wisely
To understand that wealth is money
knowledge and wisdom
To bear fruits of labor

To share with you, and your children
and your children's children
I'm looking at the forest and not the trees
So please forgive me

Believe some days I remain sad
I'm not a Dead Beat Dad
I'm a Dead Broke Dad

In quest of a dream I had

THE POWER 2

Love is unexplainable
Love is a miracle
Love is unchangeable
Love is a spiritual connection with an angel's reflection
Love has been here just as long as GOD has
Love is the future, present and past
Love is right between your soul and spirit, that speaks
only for your ear inside to hear it

Love is the magnet for soul mates
Love is the key to the pearly gates
Love is synonymous to all living beings and things

Love is a photograph of the non-living
Love is experiencing, receiving and giving
Love is a wonderful feeling
Love is healing
Love doesn't hurt
Love is what makes everything work
Love is the heart of forgiveness
Love is the cure for any sickness

Love doesn't discriminate
Love is the savior
Love is a life saver
Love keeps the world together

JOHNNY E. OSBY II

Love shines in any weather
Love makes smart folks turn foolish

How to love one on one
was never taught in my school
So how does one learn to love
Close your mouth
open your ears and delete your fears
envision love crystal clear

VACATION

Fresh out the tub cleansed of all your worldly ways
I dare to stare at your beauty blinding like sunrays
I gaze over your glazed body
watching isolated beads of water
on something so godly

Taking the initiative to tour your curving ass
Body exposed and vulnerable to the one eye
that never closes

Anything goes
A sexual carnival
Up down, around and around
Straight and back
Up high and on the ground
Sweat, saliva and secretions are one
on each tongue

The night's young but exhausted from dual orgasms
which produced ill faces and back spasms
Arched backs and curled toes
Retardation effect…lay back…inhale the moment
Anticipate the next episode
To be continued…

LANDSCAPING

I see a lot of women seeking relationships
but not equipped with the proper tools
to keep up the maintenance

Most of you stop educating yourselves after your high
school diplomas, G.E.Ds and college degrees

For the record…knowledge is infinite
Love and life are too broad to fill the classroom
First of all your work ethics need to evolve
to answer problems sex can't solve

And when sex is involved
please don't let your stomach become
bigger than your breast
Never the less…that's a demonstration
of your work ethics
Nutritional and physical values
works within the soul and strengthen your spirit

You wonder why your soul mate called
and you couldn't hear it
There's a lot boys looking like men in disguise
There's a lot of girl friends frontin' like wives
History lesson…what's your
moms past relationships like

THE WINDOWS TO MY SOUL

Most of the time it's what
your relationships will be like
if you don't break the negative cycle
Compatibility, chemistry, up bringing, dreams
and goals play and important part

Willie Lynch fathered your roles as mothers
to smother a brother leaving his manhood covered
Once a man stood discovered he became an enemy/lover

What are your short, mid and long term goals
Do you shop at the organic grocery store
Do you read the back of food labels to see what you
feeding me, you and your kids

If I happen to get sick can you run the family business
Can we talk assets, interest rates and liabilities
instead of the rent's late…I need…
and did you pay the utilities

When will you women understand
your definition of a man is not a man
How can you fully understand if I'm a man still learning

When did you perfect your role as women to have
enough time to critique my learning
Nature doesn't program for failure
When a real man presents himself you will submit
And he'll guide you to heaven and back round-trip

BLACK X-MAS

A merry X-mas is a holiday to worship
A white Pagan idol that bears gifts for everyone

I was told by Christians that it is the
birthday for the chosen one
Logically speaking how could any one document such a
miraculous event by a calendar that was man-made
Not to mention worshipping an idol on the same day

A merry X-mas is a very profitable
day for economics in general
People say love is love and not based on material
so why are you spending your rent money
on toys and meaningful gifts
That's not adult-like and responsible is it…

A merry X-mas is status quo
Its actually sad and a reminder for
those that don't have dough

So we over-compensate by giving a lot of gifts
Then I see you at the check cashing line pissed
Knowing your capabilities is a part of being grown
so if you can't handle being Queen or King please by any
means get off the throne

THE WINDOWS TO MY SOUL

Don't get me wrong I like the holiday for the family's
togetherness and festive vibe
But then I remember this holiday is based on a lie
Family togetherness we can do any
time we choose to

We'd rather wait for sad occasions like
Memorial Day
The 4th of U lie…excuse me July
Labor Day
Thanksgiving
X-mas
and funerals

The best gift has been taken for granted for years
It's called…LIFE
Lets practice celebrating LIFE as a major
holiday and why we're here
We wouldn't need sad reminders
GOD, FAMILY, LIFE and LOVE
is enough for me so every day's a celebration see
Research what you're celebrating and what you're
celebrating for

Merry_____fill in what you're really celebrating

JOHNNY E. OSBY II

CHILD SUPPORT $350.66

Bonding
Values
Morals
Participation
Generational stability
History
Culture
Entrepreneurship
Love
Spirituality
Leaving a Legacy

PRICELESS

Problem Solved

Pass a law to give joint custody to the parents at birth

THE WINDOWS TO MY SOUL

STEP DAD

I don't know how to be a step-dad
I am a father
Don't expect me to buy clothes
shoes and give support
without whippin' ass

I'm not a step-dad
I am a father
Don't expect me to be a friend to a
child to win you over
I d rather be hard on my kids than life
It's more beneficial when they get older

How do you tell another man to stop doing
certain things with his child that's not right
I'm not a step-dad

I was accused of showing favoritism
to my own children
How can you not if you love like I do
Why should I feel guilty
when my love is true

I spoil my children 'cause I can whip them
It goes hand and hand
Discipline is a form of love

JOHNNY E. OSBY II

BABY BROTHER

Baby brother
Get up…Get out…Get something
Aren't you tired of sleeping on the couch

I'm trying to build a family here
but it's hard with another man giving my sons
the wrong perception of what a man is about

I know people get down on their luck
I've been there but overstaying
your welcome is quite clear
Off and on for ten years strong
Something is wrong
with this family portrait

I had to leave to keep your sister from choosing
I couldn't take it any more I was losing
Blood thicker than water
I respect her for that forever and a day
She chose you over family
A hell of a decision to make

So understand what you have and
stop taking her for granted
I love you like a brother

THE WINDOWS TO MY SOUL

However I can't respect you as a man
I can care less about your situation
yet I'm raising a young man

His future depends on what he sees
So if not for me…for him…teach him

Show him the man
you would like him to be

DREAM

DREAMS
are worth me
DREAMS
are worth you
DREAMS
are worth he
DREAMS
are worth she
DREAMS
are worth truth
DREAMS
are worth what makes us believe
DREAMS
are the formation of the Earth, us, animals and trees
DREAMS
are small pieces to one big Miracle
DREAMS
are right between faith and something spiritual
DREAMS
are what makes life worth living
DREAMS
are our children
DREAMS
are plentiful enough for each of us to have thousands

DREAMS

THE WINDOWS TO MY SOUL

can come to Castles
Jail
Mansions
Houses
Prison and Public Housing
The only excuse for you not to capture a DREAM
is the fear of not having the power to believe
You can achieve
That DREAM

DREAMS are reality
Life has no sequels
Go ahead and capture you a DREAM
You deserve it!

That's my DREAM

SUNDAY DINNER

There is nothing like
playing all day and riding your bike
and coming home to Sunday dinner
that's been cooking before you left
Mamas and grand mamas' are certified soul food chefs
Greens in the sink waiting to get rinsed
Chicken in the oven baking enticing the smell sense
while I sneak to steal a piece of cheese
from the macaroni
Holding a lonely piece of bologna
to tie me down until dinners done
as I ride off with my friend to have a little fun
who's mom that doesn't cook like mine
Your mom is cool he replied
At play
all I could think of was Sunday Dinner on display
Visualizing my plate before and after
playing around with mom and my step dad with laughte
I went home early that day
anticipating dinner plus I had school the next day
Riding home fast as I could
through alleys and past the woods
Put my bike in the basement and wash my hands
Food smelling delicious as
mom and step dad sing and dance
Johnnie Taylor I think while I fixed my plate

THE WINDOWS TO MY SOUL

mouth watering corn bread golden brown
don't forget the potato salad mom yelled
I heard every sound
I sat down at the table
but forgot my fork
I opened the drawer
grabbed a fork and a cup
began to pour
some kool aid
Orange and lemonade mix
my favorite
A burp followed soon after I finished
Mom that's was gooood
Gave my dog the bones

That's Sunday Dinner in my hood.

THE HUSTLE

Though I have many options
when it comes to the hustle my options are slim
Either do it or don't and end up like them
Living day to day check to check with out any time for
myself family or friends
That lifestyle is okay I guess
yet there is hardly room for progress
Me I rather be boarding a private jet in Miami
So I keep my nose to the dirt and my ear to the street
Fear is obsolete
Hustling octopus style y'all see me
Three world's past reality
My vision is measured on GOD's speed
Don't believe in luck
I believe in Fate Purpose Destiny
so my destination is only fit for me a King I be
It takes time to learn different lessons to advance
to the next land
Sort of like adventurous video games
you playing
Stop playing life is serious
but you not
Take back control on your life
by staying in tuned to the Most High….GOD
Exploit your gifts and supply jobs

THE REVOLUTION

Everybody fights for something
Women fight for equality, independence, quality time,
child support...etc.
Women are fighting
Men fight for more money, respect, custodial rights,
racial prejudices...etc.
Men are fighting
Gangsters fight or even kill for territory, money, drugs,
reputation...etc.
Gangsters are fighting
Hustlers are fighting for a lifestyle, a better way to make
money faster, longer...etc.
Hustlers are fighting
No one is fighting or killing for our race, our family, our
children, a better place
As we continue to be exploited, misused, abused, raped
(mentally and physically) misrepresented, brainwashed,
hung (culturally and historically), underpaid and
overworked, misguided (spiritually and politically)
Everybody fights for something

What are you fighting for...

I DO

I have not
found a woman
who knows her
self-purpose
or GOD
Therefore
I have not
found my wife…

LAZY BLACK MEN

Society and black women
says that black men are lazy
That's not only insane that's crazy
I was sold and packed like sardines
in an unsanitary boat
to float across water for days and weeks
After battling in a tribal war in my homeland
dealing with an instantaneous state of shock
and never again to see my family
Watching men and women end their lives
in the Middle Passage
Voluntarily and involuntarily due to the weight of the
freight I was stripped of my culture
history and clothes
Exposed to unrecognized land
no money, home or food
I'm still the strongest man on the land
was put to work to build the home of the brave and land
of the FREE
Brave yes FREE no
Even my FREE labor was priced
The only thing I had left was mind, body and soul
and at times they were sold
Society and black women
say that black men are lazy
There is no difference today

inflation risen 20 times faster than employment raises
Correctional facilities have 80%
of Black men among them
We are the most strongest and
feared humans on this planet
Granted mental shackles keeps me stranded
and my body branded like cattle
I remember when a Black woman was
the black man's back-bone
heir to the throne
now-a-days when you come home
there's no respect, no trust, no honesty, no honor, no love
no dinner
no kisses
no hugs
no clean clothes
no back rubs
no spiritual or intellectual conversation
no motivation
no growing situation
no self-development
and no understanding on why you were sent

And they say Black men are lazy
It's human nature for you to nurture the children…lady!!

MIRACLE PROVIDERS

Women are port holes
to the spiritual realm to adhere
Light, food and air
to incubate a predestined miracle

A warrior, soldier, king, queen, prophet or philosopher
Their body evolves to accommodate these miracles
At this stage many feel insecure and not sure
but the security of the miracle is so pure

Their bodies glistens with a celestial glow
Protection surrounds her anywhere she goes
Everyone knows

There is a miracle amongst their vicinity
Inside the womb she bears the most sacred characteristic
of the extraordinary entity

Her attraction multiplies like repetitive
equals on a calculator
Her appetites greater
intriguing with various combinations

Pickles and peanut butter
ranch dressing and potato chips
The supreme queen

JOHNNY E. OSBY II

The pinnacle of regal

Your wish is my command
360 degrees is a full circle which equals 9
as well as the months it takes to obtain
mortality so divine
To proceed on their mission
for all mankind

THE WINDOWS TO MY SOUL

MY PRAYER

GOD I would like to thank you for
blessing me with my gifts
which includes vision allowing me to bring
your will and purpose to the people
I would also like to ask that you give me
understanding and wisdom not only
life in general but some of the passages I have written
Please continue to bless those less fortunate
and on the wrong path
Guide them back to their dreams
I would like to acknowledge spirits that left prematurely
before finishing their mission
Also welcome them back to continue their quest of
finishing their mission
I would like to acknowledge ancestors and elders not
here that are accountable for my spirit and for my
presence here on earth.
Especially those lost in the
Middle Passage and the Holocaust
Thank you for directing instrumental beings along my
path to put me back on track when I was off and lost
Thank you for my family, friends and associates
and thank you for my life

Ashe…Harambe !!!

LIVE

The U.S Department of Welfare tracked 100 people from the ages of twenty to sixty five years of age (retirement) and documented it.

36 were dead
54 were living on government or family support
5 were still working
4 were well off
1 was wealthy

Excluding weekends over 95% of the population spends half their life by age sixty five sleeping (six hours a day) working (eight hours a day) quality time with children or spouse (four hours a day).

<u>Are you really grown</u>? As an infant till 18 years of age, the average person depended on their parents for food, shelter, decision making and money. Then after age 18 some went to college, not only for additional knowledge and degrees, but to fill a void or role parents had which was food, shelter, decision making and money. Finally at 22 a graduation from college with a degree for a job or career, now there are bills for homes, cars, children and nice jewelry. So they're GROWN right? *Wrong,* because they are still dependant on their jobs as they were their parents for food, shelter, decision making and money. S

in conclusion those that think they're grown think again.
They'll be grown once they reach financial freedom.
Freedom of time without having to ask their parents,
school, or job/career for permission to go anywhere
If you choose to go to Jamaica for a week you can and
come back with money waiting for you
People start your own small business
if not for yourselves
do it for your children
NOW THAT'S BEING GROWN!

Ladies and Gentlemen
we only have one life to live
Live it to the fullest and never settle for anything less
than the best for you and your situation
Live life
There are no sequels

Life is beautiful if you understand it

PIMPIN

What is pimpin
Pimpin is having a child
and getting on Section 8 (free housing)

What is pimpin
Pimpin is having a child/baby daddy
and getting on welfare (free food)

What is pimpin
Pimpin is having a child
and getting a utility voucher (free utilities)

What is pimpin
Pimpin is having a child
and living with the Baby Daddy (free?)

What is pimpin
Pimpin is having a child with all this free shit
with a job and filing child support on your baby's daddy
with another niggah calling.......THAT'S PIMPIN

BLIND FAITH

Blind faith is walking in a direction
unaware of where it's leading
however somehow knowing when you'll
get there

BLIND FAITH

Is doing something now and finding
out five years later what you were doing it for

BLIND FAITH

Is two people falling in love
getting married and
growing old together

BLIND FAITH

Is taking a risk or a chance
although it's really not a risk or chance
cause your life plans are in GODS hands

BLIND FAITH

JOY RIDING

The majority of people
love joy riding
Get in the car start it up
shift into park
pass neutral
pass reverse
to drive
Without any destination in mind
just driving
Gas gage is broken
unaware of how
much gas you have left to know how far you can drive
Just driving
bypassing many beautiful people, things and ways
just driving
Just as you think about a destination…you run out of ga
just driving

Park - planning
Neutral - meditation/prayer
Reverse - past/history
Driving - plans in motion
Destination - purpose
Gas - Life

WHAT I'M BREATHING

It's less than 20% of oxygen left in the air

which leaves 80%

What am I breathing

They cutting down the Rain Forest and not replanting

Depleting our major oxygen source

Question how low

can the percentage go

before we suffocate ourselves

What am I breathing

There are more cars on the road

and more factories to exploit our people (slavery)

Releasing toxins by the gallons

What am I breathing

What am I breathing

What am I breathing

Exhaust smoke

chemical smoke

tobacco smoke

smog

Free radicals

Oh yea…and oxygen

that's what I'm breathing

COMPANY

I was feeling on top of my game
in all ways
Been waiting for this date for many days
We conversed on how she loved company
and how she was so lonely
I felt almost sad
In hand I had
flowers and bubbly
The night was perfect
Repeated it for weeks and months
Things started to change after months turned into years
and happiness turned into tears
I ask what's wrong but she couldn't answer
She told me to go she'd became my cancer
She diseased my spirit
The only unknown mystery
I remember when she said
I love company
but I had to leave
my beloved misery

IDENTITY CRISIS

I saw you at the welfare office
asking for help
I also saw you at the club with a Gucci purse
and matching belt

I saw you rolling an Escalade on dubs
then I overheard you saying you live at home with your
mom on the corner of Dowannabe and Scrubs

There's no problem with wanting more
but handle your priorities
and your capabilities
Stop trying to be something you are not
and living outside your means
That's a sure fire way to keep you
from living your dreams
Be content for what you are able to do
Perfect it and move on to something new
If you're broke
be broke
If you're poor
be poor
Don't be ashamed
Only be ashamed if you're broke and poor and not doing
a DAMN THANG to get more.

THE WINDOWS TO MY SOUL

KARMA

Why do you hate us so much…why
Can you explain what we did as a race
to make you treat us this way…why
Dating back to Egypt
what did we do historically
that made you destroy our history our culture
our self worth our humanity our dignity
our truth our mystery our proof
Such knowledge we gave and was stripped of yet you
treat us worst than dogs...why

What did we do to you
Even to this day nothing has change
We still get treated the same just a different era different
method different way different game
You've condition my children to think anything black is
bad that includes the skin
there in that's sad……why

What did we do to you
Do explain what ever it is
We'll never do it again
but then again if we knew you were going
to treat us this way
we should have done something instead of sitting there
while you're killing our people physically and

psychologically slowly

Our children are caught in the middle
Why are you doing this
it can't be 'cause GOD said so
Karma will be the wrath
so are you ready when
Karma crosses your path…

THE WINDOWS TO MY SOUL

GOD DAMN!

When I loved you
I didn't have enough money

When I tried to get enough money
I didn't spend enough time

When I started to spend time with you
I didn't take you out enough

When I took you out
I didn't pay you enough attention

When I paid you enough attention I was broke
and striving to live life better
which takes time and effort

That took away from our relationship
I wish I could give all that you ask
but I can't
All I ask from you is your understanding
and support…thanks!

COMEDIC TIMING

Life is a funny thing
Sometimes the right decision
brings on the wrong reaction

It's so hard to make the right decision
yet so easy to make the wrong decision

Society and black women always
question a black man's masculinity

The funny thing is
neither one of them is a black man
in my hood

THE WINDOWS TO MY SOUL

NUMBER EIGHT SIDE WAYS

Knowledge is infinite

Space is infinite

Numbers are infinite

Spirituality is infinite

God is infinite

Dreams are infinite

Therefore your vision is infinite

Remove the box
and seek knowledge and truth

Experience real freedom

Don't be afraid to research everything
including religion

IT'S FREE!!!

STRANGE FRUIT

I was walking upon an old country road
in Montgomery, Alabama
young and innocent
far from being old
Sun blazin' birds chirpin' fruit bloomin'
tree after tree
as the smell of summer turned
into a piercing stench of death
I began to see
with a loss of breath
a strange fruit

THE WINDOWS TO MY SOUL

UNIDENTIFIED ANGEL

Sometimes I look inside my memory
to remember those that died
and what they meant to me

Thinking how I took them for granted and
wishing I could bring them back single handed

Everything has a purpose
I used to get scared when I felt spirits surface

Now I realize they assist in guiding me
as long as I stay in tune
they will never die to me

It seems as if death is like the lottery
when your number pops up its time to s
ay good bye to me

This goes out to every one who has
or will lose a loved one
As a reminder to love
each and every day
because you never know if it's your time to go

This is not intended to make one sad
but to make one glad

JOHNNY E. OSBY II

You had the pleasure of meeting an unidentified angel
among your path

R.I.P

James Carter
Jamie Antoine
Mom and Pop Vickers
Markie Jones
Mahogany
Ben Lash
Pop Larkins
Barney Holiday
Steve Warren
Sean Moss
Torrey
Richard Lylard
Meechie

GIFTS

Gifts
are like animals
Each animal has some
type of survival tactic
Birds have wings
Lions have agility
Elephants have strength
Each human was created
with the same intent
Find your gift
and survive

TRUE STORY

You always want
the opposite
of what you
don't have
instead of appreciating
what you do have

THE WINDOWS TO MY SOUL

IT'S ALWAYS THE MAN'S FAULT

If a woman cheats
then it's the man fault for not taking the time needed for
her

If a man cheats
then he's being the no good dog women
proclaim him to be

If a woman doesn't work
then it's up to the man to pay all the bills

If a man doesn't work
then he's a lazy ass, irresponsible, immature man that
doesn't accept responsibility

If a man sits back and endures the criticism is he a man?

If a man leaves
then he has abandoned his family

If a woman leaves
then the man must have driven her away

If a man dreams
then he's wasting time

If a woman dreams
then she's independent and strong

If a woman can't pay child support
then the child's dad's not paying enough

If a man can't pay child support
then he's a dead beat

If a woman stays with a man for the sake of family
then she's strong

If a man stays with a woman for the sake of family
then he's wrong

THE WINDOWS TO MY SOUL

LETTER TO MAMA

Dear Mama

I would like to take the time to
immortalize my love to you before it's too late
I know I haven't been the perfect child
but better late than never to tell you how great
you were in raising me

I have absolutely no regrets for
what life has given to me
You taught me that optimistically
grazing the surface of this beautiful planet taking the
time to see as much as I can within my budget

You gotta love it!

Life is the halftime show to eternity
so I'm trying to enjoy every moment of it
but something is burning in me
I want the best for all within my immediate circle
but my hustle isn't working fast enough for you

The more time I take the more gray your hair gets
which takes you closer to eternity
A place I've only seen once
before I got here

There's so many things I want to do for myself
you and my children before I return there
Though time has a hold on you I continue to try to
manipulate time by getting the annual
salary of a man 55 by the time I'm 35

A lot of people close to me have doubted me
but not you mama…other than my kids
I live for you
I want to be able to show you things
you can dream about and not dream of
So if time just so happens to hug you before I do
then I'm going to express my love and hugs
before time does
Just one lifetime of loving you mama
won't be long enough
therefore I had some children to relay the message
to the generations coming after us
to let them know how wonderful you are and how much
influence you have on their lives

I know I'm not that emotional when it comes to
expressing my feelings in person, but God gave me the
gift to express them on paper…to immortalize them
forever

With all my love
Your son, Big John

THE WINDOWS TO MY SOUL

LOST AND FOUND

Its hard to find a woman
that knows herself inside and out
ad knows where she's going and stays on the right route

Her place is solidified in the spiritual community
She knows her place at home without immunity
so keeping an eye on politics to see what they're trying
to do to me

She assists and leads when needed
She prays for me at night when my soul has weaken
She rubs my back when my chest is inflated
encourages my spirit when I think I cant make it

She fills my stomach with the proper nutrients
Ier sexual ambiance gives me a lifetime vacation in 30
minute segments

Her actions hypnotizes me to never cheat
A match made in Heaven...predestined on Earth

Never had to question whether or not it'll work
We work together
All the money on Earth
could not match her value or worth

JOHNNY E. OSBY II

INSTITUTIONALIZED

When we refer to being institutionalized
we think of being incarcerated
Institutions are very under rated
I've never been in Prison
however I have been institutionalized
all my life

The day I started pre-school to headstart
elementary to middle school
high school to college
I found they were all forms of institutions

With correctional officers/teachers
dictating and manipulating our thoughts
emotions and purpose
Teachers are the most influential component in our
scholastic and academic development

The catch is
most of them are European
which is not good for those of us
that are of African descent
Due to racial tension, competition and oppression we ar
being guided…

THE WINDOWS TO MY SOUL

Besides prison the other best way to control
a strong man is spiritually
Yes churches are institutions as well
Churches are spiritual liquor stores

So in conclusion we are all institutionalized
Prisoners of some sort
Realize and grow and know
why and who's institutionalizing you

FAMILY REUNION

How you doing…
I haven't seen you since you were three
I used to change your diapers boy
This your cousin
Do you remember her
Yeah y'all was little
You then grew up to be a fine young man
So handsome
I heard you were in college
That's your Uncle right there
You want something to eat
How many kids do you have now
How's your mom doing
Time sure does fly
What are you doing for yourself now
Boy you look just like your father
Are you one of the pall bearers for
Big Momma's Funeral tomorrow

Yes ma'am

THE WINDOWS TO MY SOUL

MY NAME IS...FOREVER

My brain processes thoughts three
times the speed of God
To put dreams into my bloodline
five generations from now

So they may visit my struggle and compare maps of
roads already driven on
With foot prints, tire tracks and occasional hands
so I may fossilize the hour glass sands

Leaving moments that disturbs the devils sleep
and tell the truth about God
and why he embedded racism in us to destroy our lives
I turned my back with the strength of ten angels
thirty giants and multiple spirits
with a manuscript of papyrus paper called the Maat

I've acknowledge my intelligence is beyond this
atmosphere

So I choose to speak to a few before I'm out of here
Though I'm still here
my words are me...FOREVER...So FOREVER
I'll be

If God didn't say it...there's some imperfection in it

THE PROJECTS

The projects consist of
stock brokers
real estate developers
business moguls
authors
artists
poets
politicians
professional athletes
community icons
inventors
musicians
philosophers etc.

The projects make some of us
dependant
unproductive
unmotivated
lifetime consumers
lifetime laborers
alcoholics…drug addicts…drug dealers
restricted prisoners

Live in the projects…don't become a project!

THE WINDOWS TO MY SOUL

HOSPITALITY

I embrace my children's future
like a scared mother protecting her son from the world
I see things only the year 3015 historians know
My inner zeal supercedes the cosmos
leaving shadows on Mars and surrounding stars

Knowledge and space are infinite
however I count nine planets every 2100 years
So by the time the year 4200 arrives
there shall be eighteen

Humans are more than a million years old
The feeling of control erases accurate history

Truth has no mystery
Language lacks a lot of the untold viciously
Life and Death is a mathematical
equation to measure time
Since we try to measure time
we lose life
and since we lose life
we anticipate death
Before us is God
After us is God
There is no in between
There is only God

JOHNNY E. OSBY II

No one knows the truth but God
Life multiplying at the speed of light
could not acquire the truth

Those that say they do
lie with a honest demeanor

Deceased presidents configure morals for value
Spiritual satellites selling Gods broadcast to the masses
Everyone's entitled to fruits of labor
So when does one have enough fruit

Religion is a systematic way of categorizing
Religiously I follow my purpose

If one race has control
do you think they will honestly release control
or happily give control to another race to be controlled

I'm just an artist with a piece of paper as big as the worl

With one number two pencil with no eraser
Welcome to my home
My home is yours

THE WINDOWS TO MY SOUL

GRAPHIC DESIGN

The strength of a man is often measured by his criminal
record, credit score and economic stature
by society and potential wives

How dare you forget we are the most feared, most
penalized by lies

This doesn't justify those that are unjustifiable
By design we are stripped of all valuables
fathers included

Secluded and formed by the streets
curbs being my closest relative

When I'm lost I'm feared
Help is not an option

So sex, money and drugs enlarges life's buzz
Near death situations

Death is near
death fears nothing just like me
Hugs are foreign
doesn't speak my language
so I make the best out of my anguish
I am not a Thug,

JOHNNY E. OSBY II

I am a man labeled as one
because I don't fall into societies plans
never have…never will
not until they kill me
But that's society's initial plan all along…Damn!
It's by design
What doesn't kill me makes me stronger
and what don't heal me I need no longer

Everyone thinks I'm better off dead
I have the strength to go against the grain to get fed
See I know time is short
plus in certain areas they kill, beat and set up Black Men
like myself for sport
or release me to my children's mother who threatens to
call the court

You know, parole officer and/or child support
loving to control me
See it's by design

I don't know my mother…Africa
but I do know my father…slavery
Run niggah and find peace
was the best advice he ever gave to me

THE WINDOWS TO MY SOUL

VAGINA

You are the most powerful woman on the planet
You are the drug to all men
supply and demand
I demand it

Men pay a hell of price to have you
monetarily and involuntarily

You know the secret you keep amongst your society
a sorority of women with different priorities

Some use you for good
others for evil
some for survival
some for their people

Civilizations population depend on you
that's why there is so much power in you

Sometimes I find myself pacing for your fix
You know this

So I can't understand why you play so many tricks
Your overseer exploits your talents for authorization to
break me down
to become lame for you

JOHNNY E. OSBY II

Now you've crossed the line
I am a niggah
I got game for you

In classical Virginia I was referred to as a stud
every time I was shipped to town they lined them up
It's in my blood

As you know there are different varieties
however you plus me made some type of magic
That's why I crave for you singing a song called
"I gotta have it"

Somewhere down the road you use your
magic for the wrong reason
What a tragic our magic no longer breathing
My divine blueprint overrides unnecessary data
You took away the magic

Vagina you don't even matter
See part of becoming a man is knowing how to control
your urge
I am purged of you
How could you
use something so miraculous for personal fame

I thought we were a team
unified like a body of water
now we're just steam remodeling the harbor

MY MOTHER

I AM
the second largest continent on this planet

I AM
the richest continent on this planet
at produced the first man, woman and child to walk this
land

I AM
ared by all conspired predators who kill my children for
my natural resources
They steal and kill then lie with honesty, a very
disturbing enemy to have

I AM
married to God so therefore you're going to feel the
wrath when my husband gets home
I've watch you steal and rape my culture, language,
knowledge, wisdom and religion
for CAPITALISM

ou've flooded my history literally psychologically and
physically
Segregated my children conclusively from your
evolvement
A billion lies cannot stop the penetration of truth

Technology imprisons ingenuity and over sees my
knowledge seeking
Kemet been broken down to water
down colleges seeking
tuition but my intuition is more
valuable than your institution

Languages are one of the vast
gateways to acquiring the truth

Hieroglyphics is a form of language
but there is no indigenous people left for proof

How can you dictate what a word is when you've
created words from various languages

There is no limit on creativity
so I watch and cry diamonds as you steal my tears
to industrialize my pain for symbols of love

All countries against me yet I'm still strong enough
to call for my children
to protect and rescue me their Mother Africa
Until my Husband gets home

*"THIS COUNTRY IS NOT BUILT FOR US, UNLESS W
ARE BUILDING IT"*

Yin and Yang

MY PURPOSE MY DESTINY

hnny Osby resided in Akron, Ohio and has been a
tive there for the majority of his life.

well renowned entrepreneur and community icon, he
s developed many organizations and businesses here in
: area in hopes to help revitalize and rebuild the
rican American community and family as well.

hnny has four beautiful children, and a host of family
d friends. His spirit is well loved as a self-made
naissance man. He has made an impact and difference
the African American Community.

the near but distant future, he looks forward to having
street honored in his name "Johnny E Osby II" Blvd.

: personifies motivation for his beliefs, rituals and
termination to become a better well rounded person.

ith continuous self development and personal growth,
; legacy will definitely be a prominent force now and
rever.

ith his children, music, poetry, drawings, and comedic
rious personality, he work s by his passion through non
rbal illustrations of blue collar work ethics.

He will continue to finish what he started: *a "Revolutio of Legacies"*

He bids you God speed!

CPSIA information can be obtained at www.ICGtesting.com
Printed in the USA
BVOW082124260712

296140BV00001BA/1/P